FISHERMAN
BIBLE STUDYGUIDES

SONG
of
SONGS

A Dialogue of Intimacy

JAMES REAPSOME

D1407676

SHAW BOOKS
an imprint of WATERBROOK PRESS

Song of Songs
A SHAW BOOK
PUBLISHED BY WATERBROOK PRESS
2375 Telstar Drive, Suite 160
Colorado Springs, Colorado 80920
A division of Random House, Inc.

ISBN 0-87788-826-4

Printed in the United States of America
2002—First Edition

10 9 8 7 6 5 4 3 2 1

Contents

How to Use This Studyguide

Fisherman studyguides are based on the inductive approach to Bible study. Inductive study is discovery study; we discover what the Bible says as we ask questions about its content and search for answers. This is quite different from the process in which a teacher *tells* a group *about* the Bible—what it means and what to do about it. In inductive study, God speaks directly to each of us through his Word.

A group functions best when a leader keeps the discussion on target, but the leader is neither the teacher nor the "answer person." A leader's responsibility is to *ask*—not *tell*. The answers come from the text itself as group members examine, discuss, and think together about the passage.

There are four kinds of questions in each study. The first is an *approach question*. Asked and answered before the Bible passage is read, this question breaks the ice and helps you start thinking about the topic of the Bible study. It begins to reveal where thoughts and feelings need to be transformed by Scripture.

Some of the earlier questions in each study are *observation questions*—who, what, where, when, and how—designed to help you learn some basic facts about the passage of Scripture.

Once you know what the Bible says, you need to ask, *What does it mean?* These *interpretation questions* help you discover the writer's basic message.

Next come *application questions*, which ask, *What does it mean to me?* They challenge you to live out the Scripture's life-transforming message.

Fisherman studyguides provide spaces between questions for jotting down responses as well as any related questions you would like to raise in the group. Each group member should have a copy of the studyguide and may take a turn in leading the group.

A group should use any accurate, modern translation of the Bible such as the *New International Version,* the *New American Standard Bible,* the *New Living Translation,* the *New Revised Standard Version,* the *New Jerusalem Bible,* or the *Good News Bible.* (Other translations or paraphrases of the Bible may be referred to when additional help is needed.) Bible commentaries should not be brought to a Bible study because they tend to dampen discussion and keep people from thinking for themselves.

Suggestions for Group Leaders

1. Thoroughly read and study the Bible passage before the meeting. Get a firm grasp on its themes and begin applying its teachings for yourself. Pray that the Holy Spirit will "guide you into all truth" (John 16:13) so that your leadership will guide others.

2. If any of the studyguide's questions seem ambiguous or unnatural to you, rephrase them, feeling free to add others that seem necessary to bring out the meaning of a verse.

3. Begin (and end) the study promptly. Start by asking someone to pray that every participant will both understand the passage and be open to its transforming power. Remember, the Holy Spirit is the teacher, not you!

4. Ask for volunteers to read the passages aloud.

5. As you ask the studyguide's questions in sequence, encourage everyone to participate in the discussion. If some are silent, try gently suggesting, "Let's have an answer from someone who hasn't spoken up yet."

6. If a question comes up that you can't answer, don't be afraid to admit that you're baffled. Assign the topic as a research project for someone to report on next week, or say, "I'll do some studying and let you know what I find out."

7. Keep the discussion moving, but be sure it stays focused. Though a certain number of tangents are inevitable, you'll want to quickly bring the discussion back to the topic at hand. Also, learn to pace the discussion so that you finish the lesson in the time allotted.

8. Don't be afraid of silences; some questions take time to answer, and some people need time to gather courage to speak. If silence persists, rephrase your question, but resist the temptation to answer it yourself.

9. If someone comes up with an answer that is clearly illogical or unbiblical, ask for further clarification: "What verse suggests that to you?"

10. Discourage overuse of cross references. Learn all you can from the passage at hand, while selectively incorporating a few important references suggested in the studyguide.

11. Some questions are marked with a ✐. This indicates that further information is available in the Leader's Notes at the back of the guide.

12. For further information on getting a new Bible
    study group started and keeping it functioning
    effectively, read *You Can Start a Bible Study Group*
    by Gladys Hunt and *Pilgrims in Progress: Growing
    Through Groups* by Jim and Carol Plueddemann.
    (Both books are available from Shaw Books).

Suggestions for Group Members

1. Learn and apply the following ground rules for
   effective Bible study. (If new members join the
   group later, review these guidelines with the whole
   group.)

2. Remember that your goal is to learn all that you can
   from the Bible passage being studied. Let it speak for
   itself without using Bible commentaries or other
   Bible passages. There is more than enough in each
   assigned passage to keep your group productively
   occupied for one session. Sticking to the passage
   saves the group from insecurity ("I don't have the
   right reference books—or the time to read anything
   else.") and confusion ("Where did *that* come from?
   I thought we were studying _____.").

3. Avoid the temptation to bring up those fascinating
   tangents that don't really grow out of the passage
   you are discussing. If the topic is of common interest, you can bring it up later in informal conversation after the study. Meanwhile, help one another
   stick to the subject.

4. Encourage one another to participate. People
   remember best what they discover and verbalize for

themselves. Some people are naturally shy, while others may be afraid of making a mistake. If your discussion is free and friendly and you show real interest in what other group members think and feel, the quieter ones will be more likely to speak up. Remember, the more people involved in a discussion, the richer it will be.

5. Guard yourself from answering too many questions or talking too much. Give others a chance to share their ideas. If you are one who participates easily, discipline yourself by counting to ten before you open your mouth.

6. Make personal, honest applications and commit yourself to letting God's Word change you.

A Dialogue of Intimacy

L ove is as strong as death.... It burns like blazing fire, like a mighty flame. Many waters cannot quench love; rivers cannot wash it away" (Song of Songs 8:6-7).

So sang the bride to her bridegroom in Song of Songs, the Bible's picture of intimacy in marriage. Their romance flourishes emotionally and physically. Their songs carry the flush of anticipation and the excitement and satisfaction of fulfillment. Their songs sink to the valley of momentary disappointment and rise to the heights of joy and pleasure. They show us how God intended women and men to enjoy the pleasures of sexual union.

Scholars have long troubled over the exact meaning of words and phrases found in this Old Testament book, many of which appear nowhere else in the Bible. One commentator has devoted 140 pages to the problems of interpretation alone and calls it a "brief sketch." Scholars have also struggled with the poetic forms, trying to make them fit some logical outline, but Song of Songs eludes such precision. Emotions, not carefully reasoned arguments, carry these songs.

We study this book because the apostle Paul declared, "All Scripture is God-breathed and is useful for teaching, rebuking, correcting and training in righteousness" (2 Timothy 3:16), and because the Lord Jesus Christ said that we must live by every word from God (Matthew 4:4). Although Song of Songs is not a marriage manual, it nevertheless instructs us in the value of intimacy. It is a poetic dialogue between lovers, accompanied by occasional choruses from onlookers. In our study we must allow poetic license to overcome our natural propensity to put everything—even love—under a microscope. Song of Songs allows us to luxuriate with two people who are madly in love with each other. Their dazzling liberty with words and feelings sets our own dry relationships on fire and rebukes our maudlin, sex-as-appetite approach to lovemaking.

"No other book of the Bible is so thick with simile, metaphor, and other artful examples of language," cites the *Dictionary of Biblical Imagery* (Ryken, Wilhoit, and Longman, general eds., Downers Grove, Ill.: InterVarsity, 1998, p. 806). Therefore, we are challenged to think differently and to allow our hearts and minds to roam, and we are comforted that our ideas about the meanings of these images are as valid as the next person's. This approach will enrich group study.

In this studyguide, the thread that links each of the songs is *intimacy;* the structure is dialogue in poetic language. Song of Songs was not written to prove a psychological theory about love; however, when we read it as a dialogue between lovers, we learn about intimacy on various levels. Our chapter titles do not fit a Western outline of logical progression, but rather, they try to reflect some aspect of the songs that is incorporated in each chapter. Also, since the Bible was not written with chapter breaks, the songs are not confined to those boundaries.

Some commentaries on Song of Songs jump immediately from the love story to applications that can be made about the Christian's love affair with the Lord Jesus Christ. We chose not to do that, although, as we listen to the songs, we can easily see

New Testament parallels in the doctrines of Christ and the church.

Our prayer is that readers will be released to revel in the pure essence of human love, God's magnificent gift. We cannot be squeamish as we read and study or we will miss the beauty and transparency of these love songs. Above all, may God be praised and glorified as we try to grasp the wonders of his gift of marital bliss.

Intimacy Initiated

SONG OF SONGS 1

Solomon's book opens with an emotionally charged dialogue between the bride and the bridegroom as they anticipate the intimacy of their marriage relationship. It's like a Broadway musical production, complete with female and male stars and a supporting cast of singers—in this case, friends of the bride.

In this study we want to catch the spirit of the palace wedding. First, reflect on the joy experienced at weddings today. Then recognize that, here, we are privileged to listen to the most intimate repartee between lovers as they describe their love in the colorful imagery of King Solomon's day. Whatever else we see in this drama, we must look for important clues about how the bride and bridegroom initiated their intimacy. Read chapter 1 in one sitting and reflect on the setting and the style of the literature.

1. In what kinds of relationships do we human beings experience intimacy?

Read Song of Songs 1:1-4.

✍ 2.   How would you describe the character and purpose of this book from its title?

✍ 3.   In the bride's opening song (verses 2-4), what characteristics about her bridegroom does she celebrate?

4.   What do these characteristics help us understand about his physical and moral qualities?

✍ *Indicates further information in Leader's Notes*

5. In light of the response of her friends (verse 4b), why are weddings an opportunity for joy and praise to God, even today?

Read Song of Songs 1:5-7.

6. How does the bride describe herself? What worried her? Why?

7. In contemporary society, what concerns do young women have about their appearance? Why?

What does God value above appearance? (See 1 Samuel 16:7; 1 Peter 3:3-4.)

✐ 8. Apparently the bride was mistreated by her brothers (verse 6b), and she sought a rendezvous with her bridegroom (verse 7). Although we have no details about their courtship, we can see that the bride and bridegroom followed the customs of their day and also experienced some difficulties. As we consider courtship and dating today, what role should God play?

READ SONG OF SONGS 1:8-17.

✐ 9. What do the word pictures the bride used of her bridegroom reveal about the nature of their relationship (verses 12-14)?

What other qualities might his perfume represent to her? (See also verses 2-3a.)

10. As the dialogue between the bridegroom and the bride begins in verses 15-16, what qualities stand out?

11. Of what value is it for married partners to repeat to each other the qualities that first attracted them to each other?

♪ Reflections

12. How would you describe the relationship between the bride and bridegroom thus far? What are the strengths in their relationship? the weaknesses?

13. Does sentimentality override reality in this chapter? Why or why not?

Intimacy Refreshed

SONG OF SONGS 2

In this chapter, the bride and bridegroom have their first extended conversation. They can now express their feelings more freely than during the early days at the royal palace. Yet at this stage of their relationship, their remarks to each other are still relatively brief.

Do you notice any changes in this scene compared to the opening scene? As you read this chapter, reflect on the prevailing mood. Try to grasp the setting as well as the moods of both the bride and bridegroom as they continue their dialogue. If you are comfortable with the idea, ask a female and male member of your group to read aloud the words of the bride and bridegroom.

1. What kinds of actions lead to more intimacy in relationships? What kinds of actions put a damper on intimacy?

READ SONG OF SONGS 2:1-13.

2. What words does the bride use to describe herself in verse 1?

   In what way has her view of herself changed? (See 1:5-6.)

3. How does the bridegroom pick up on and extend the figure of speech that the bride used to describe herself (verse 2)?

4. As the bride speaks again, what picture of her bridegroom does she give in verse 3? in verse 4?

✍ 5.   What does she need and desire (verses 5-6)? Why?

✍ 6.   What does the bride say that shows she has learned the value of self-control (verse 7)?

7.   In verses 8-13, the bride speaks in a soliloquy. Describe the setting of the tryst she sings about.

What figures of speech does she use to depict her lover?

   8. What words does the bridegroom use with great effectiveness to woo the bride and refresh their intimacy (verses 10,13)?

      What power do words have to enhance and refresh relationships?

READ SONG OF SONGS 2:14-17.

   9. Verse 14 marks the end of the first cycle of longing, patience, and reward. What requests does the bridegroom make (verses 14-15)? Why?

   10. What "little foxes" work against our love relationships?

In what way(s) does our walk with God help us deal with these troublemakers?

⚲ 11.   What assurance does the bride have in her relationship with the bridegroom (verse 16)?

Reflections

12.   From your review of this chapter, what expressions of affection refresh and deepen the intimacy between the two lovers?

⚲ 13.   What do the descriptive terms of intimacy between the bride and bridegroom illustrate about the Christian's relationship to Christ?

Intimacy Desired

SONG OF SONGS 3

The bride's intense desire for intimacy with her bride-groom came to her in a dream in which she thought she had lost him. Fear often destroys intimacy. We tend to second-guess our commitments, or we worry, *What if I lose my beloved? What if I can't measure up to what's expected of me?* But as it happens with many of our own dreams, fears, and worries, the bride awoke to a glorious reality—her bridegroom's wedding procession.

1. Why do you think God created our desire for intimacy?

READ SONG OF SONGS 3:1-5.

2. If you were the producer of this stage production, how would you set the scene? What clothes would

the bride wear? What expressions would you see on her face as she searched for her bridegroom? How would the watchmen react to this distraught woman?

3. What does this dream reveal about the intensity of the bride's desire?

4. What expression—used four times—captures her feelings toward her bridegroom?

5. What contemporary plays, books, movies, or television dramas build their plots on lovers searching for each other?

✗ 6. Why does the bride take her bridegroom home (verse 4)?

✗ 7. Why do you think the repeated caution of verse 5 is necessary? (See 2:7.)

8. What can we do to help people in a sex-saturated society develop strong biblical and moral values regarding sex and marriage?

READ SONG OF SONGS 3:6-11.

✗ 9. The curtain goes down and then rises on another dramatic scene: the king's wedding procession (verse 11). What impresses you about the bridegroom, Solomon? Why?

10. What aspects of Solomon's character are captured by the poetic image of the bridegroom as warrior?

✒ 11. In verse 9, the scene shifts from war to domestic matters. What other skills does the warrior-king reveal?

12. How would this thrilling scene increase their desire for intimacy?

Reflections

13. Contrast and compare the two vastly different scenes and settings for intimacy. In what way(s) do these settings reflect real life?

14. Of what value is it to confess our fears of losing our spouses or a dear loved one? If you can, tell what it was like when you discovered that your loved one was "found," that is, safe.

Intimacy Described

SONG OF SONGS 4

T he bridegroom's song to his beloved reveals the depth of
his love for her. On their wedding night he sings of her
beauty in tones of tenderest intimacy. We can feel the joy in his
heart as he tells her how beautiful she is and how much he
desires her. His marvelous metaphors may sound crude to us,
so we need to focus on the outpourings of his emotions as he
describes the intimacy of their wedding night.

1. In today's world of depersonalization and loneliness,
   what can we do to model healthy intimacy and
   make it attractive to others?

Read Song of Songs 4:1-7.

✎ 2. What is the bridegroom's theme?

In what way(s) does this theme contribute to intimacy between him and his bride?

3. Why is it important for lovers to tell each other how beautiful they are?

✎ 4. Contrast the restrained delicacy of this poem with the grossness of many modern descriptions of sexual encounters.

What pitfalls or hindrances to holiness are created by our purely physical attractions to one another?

Read Song of Songs 4:8-11.

5. How does the bridegroom intensify his paean of praise to his bride?

6. Which of her attributes does he highlight (verses 10-11)?

7. Is the bridegroom's lavish praise of his bride likely to haunt him when reality sets in? Is any bride (or groom) so gloriously perfect? Discuss.

What sincere words of praise can we use to express our intimacy, even when our loved one can't match this description?

Read Song of Songs 4:12-16.

 8. What extended metaphor does the bridegroom use to describe his bride?

As a bride, would this description flatter you? Why?

 9. How does the bride's response contribute to their intimacy (verse 16)?

10.   Of what value would it be for engaged couples to read this chapter together? for couples married twenty-five or fifty years?

Reflections

11.   Why do you think God intended this kind of erotic poetry to be included in his Holy Word?

12.   If you are married or engaged, take some time to compose a letter, poem, or song for your beloved. How often do you say to your spouse or fiancé, "You are beautiful"?

Intimacy Anticipated

SONG OF SONGS 5

S eparations are sometimes intentional, sometimes not. Re-gardless of what causes them, if handled properly, they can be occasions that heighten the anticipation of intimacy. Out of darkness bright light gleams, and our love intensifies. So it was with Solomon and his new bride.

1. It's been said that absence makes the heart grow fonder. Do you agree or disagree? Why?

READ SONG OF SONGS 5:1-9.

✒ 2. The chapter division here breaks the emotional flow of the scene. The bridegroom responds to his bride's invitation from 4:16. How does he describe the delights of their wedding night in verse 1? (See also 4:10-11,13-14.)

3. Beginning with verse 2, we can only guess how much time has passed since the bride and bridegroom's wedding. At any rate, the honeymoon is over, and it seems that some coldness has crept into their relationship (verse 3). What causes the bride's anguish (verse 6)?

4. Stirring her anticipation, the bridegroom calls her. How does he express his affection once again?

5. How does she initially react to his call (verse 3)? Why?

6. What little things often provoke misunderstandings in marriage?

7. Finding her lover gone, the bride goes on a desperate search for him (verses 6-7). Contrast the outcome of this search with the one in 3:1-4. Why do you think the watchmen treated her differently this time?

8. How do the bride's friends respond to her charge and plea (verse 9)?

Why would their question help her anticipate intimacy?

9. When we sense coldness in a friend's courtship, engagement, or marriage, how can we find God's wisdom to ask appropriate questions?

READ SONG OF SONGS 5:10-16.

10. Summarize the bride's answer (verses 10-16). What metaphors does she use to describe her lover?

11. Why would such loving and positive thoughts of him arouse her anticipation of intimacy?

What process is at work here that is instructive for us? Discuss.

Reflections

12. He calls her *sister* (verse 1) and she calls him *friend* (verse 16). How do these words show that their intimacy transcends the purely physical?

13. What makes intimacy survive and grow in spite of cold spells in our relationships?

Intimacy Recovered

SONG OF SONGS 6

Tenderness and devotion go through emotional cycles in relationships. Not every day is as exciting as the honeymoon. One of our God-given blessings is that we can develop stronger bonds of intimacy by overcoming occasional dry relational periods. Song of Songs shows how two lovers accomplished this.

1. Couples seeking divorce often say that their marriages are boring. Good counselors help them examine their real motives. What can we do to put fresh life and sparkle back into our relationships?

Read Song of Songs 6:1-3.

 2. This scene closes with the friends' assurance that
they will help the bride search for her bridegroom
(verse 1). The lovers then find each other and
relate the joys of intimacy recovered. What figures
of speech does the bride use to describe their
encounter (verse 2)? (See also 4:16.)

 3. Why can she fully enjoy intimacy with her bridegroom (verse 3)?

 4. Compare their relationship with the following scrip-
tures. What does each passage say about God's
desire for marital intimacy?

   Genesis 2:24

Ephesians 5:21-33

1 Corinthians 7:1-7

Mark 10:1-12

Read Song of Songs 6:4-9.

5. As they recover their intimacy, the bridegroom breaks out in ecstatic song about his bride. List the things he extolled about his bride in chapters 4 and 6. What new lyrics does he add this second time? How does he emphasize both her beauty and her character?

List 1 (4:1-7)   *List 2 (6:4-9)*

6. Why does the bridegroom's song bear repeating?
    Of what value was it to the bride to hear his song
    again? Of what value was it to him to sing it again?

↗ 7. What does the bridegroom say to highlight his
      bride's uniqueness (verses 8-9)? Why was this
      necessary?

Read Song of Songs 6:10-13.

↗ 8. In what way do the troubadours in our musical
      reinforce the bridegroom's song and help him to
      rediscover intimacy (verse 10)?

↗ 9. The bridegroom responds in verses 11-12. What
      poetic images does he use to picture their reunion?

10. We hear the queen identified by her hometown in verse 13. To what do the singers call the queen? Why?

Reflections

11. What did you find especially moving about this scene? Why?

12. In the flush of romantic love, we often make great promises to each other: "There is no one like you." "I will love you forever!" What spiritual resources can we draw upon to keep our vows, our promises, and our single-minded dedication? In what ways does our culture militate against keeping marital vows?

Intimacy Fulfilled

SONG OF SONGS 7

In the book of Ecclesiastes, which was probably written by Solomon as well, the author says, "There is...a time to embrace" (3:1,5). Solomon knew what he was talking about! This song reveals how the bride and bridegroom reached deeper levels of intimacy in their sexual relationship. They sing without embarrassment about their pleasures in each other. It is refreshing that they do so without resorting to lasciviousness.

1. In today's culture, sexual expertise and ecstasy are often promoted and exploited as the gods of satisfaction. How can we accept God's blessings in marital sex without turning sex into idolatry?

READ SONG OF SONGS 7:1-9A.

2. Write a brief synopsis of the essence of what the bridegroom sings to his bride. How does his song fit the overall spirit and emotion of Song of Songs?

✐ 3. List each part of the bride's body. Compare these words with the bridegroom's song in 4:1-7. Which parts of her body does he add here?

4. How does the bridegroom conclude his praise (verse 9a)?

5. Should his song be X-rated? What differences do you see between his song and many popular songs about lovemaking?

Read Song of Songs 7:9b-13.

6. Summarize the bride's song in response. What is the heart of her song?

✒ 7. Contrast verse 10 with 2:16 and 6:3. What subtle differences in her understanding of their relationship do the bride's statements suggest?

✒ 8. How does love mature in the context of mutual submission? (See Ephesians 5:21.)

9. Who takes the initiative in verse 11? (See also 2:10-14.)

Why was the bride free to do this? What does this freedom tell us about intimacy fulfilled?

10. How does the bride entice her bridegroom to new sexual delights?

11. In what ways is love constant and yet always changing and refreshing?

Reflections

12. In what ways has this chapter helped you appreciate God's gift of sexual fulfillment as a means of achieving marital intimacy?

13. Why would it be appropriate to use Song of Songs as part of family teaching on sexual intimacy?

Intimacy Matured

SONG OF SONGS 8

This book of love songs culminates in one of the finest odes to love ever written. It is a fitting climax to this musical drama. There is also a brief flashback to childhood, which is sung by the bride's brothers. In their closing songs, the bride and bridegroom repeat earlier songs, showing that their intimacy has matured.

1. What love songs can you remember from the days of your courtship? Why did these resonate with you?

READ SONG OF SONGS 8:1-4.

✐ 2. The bride continues a song she began in 7:9b. What
image reflects her desire for greater intimacy?

In what roles does she see her bridegroom?

3. Compare the bride's cautions in 2:7, 3:5, and 8:4.
Why do you think she repeats this refrain throughout her songs?

READ SONG OF SONGS 8:5-7.

*This section begins a series of short reprises leading to the song's
conclusion. The poet introduces the final dialogue of intimacy
with a question intended to draw our attention to the lovers. The
bride sings a brief song that has been widely quoted as a superla-
tive definition of love.*

◢ 4. What request does the bride make of her bride-
       groom (verse 6)? What do his heart and arm
       represent?

       What contemporary "seals" do we use to signify the
       strength of our commitments to each other?

◢ 5. Identify each figure of speech the bride uses to
       define love (verses 6-7). Then discuss what each one
       signifies.

6. Complete the following sentences using as many of your own similes and metaphors as possible:

Love is as...

Love is like...

7. What gives love its permanence?

Why can we not buy another person's love (verse 7b)?

READ SONG OF SONGS 8:8-14.

8. Apparently the poet gave this song to the bride's brothers. It is a flashback to the days when she was at home, too young to marry. What role did her brothers play in her life?

9. In response, how does the sister show that she was properly ready for marriage and able to meet her bridegroom's needs (verses 10-12)?

10. In the closing songs of the bridegroom and the bride (verses 13-14), what does each one emphasize?

11. In what way does this poetic song show the maturity of the couple's intimacy?

12. Imagine you are now leaving the theater after having seen this biblical "musical." Describe your reactions.

REFLECTIONS

✎ 13.   As you reflect on this study, what have you discovered about God's gift of intimacy in marriage?

On what different levels of human experience did the two lovers become one?

14.   Does the Song of Songs inspire you to praise God? to commit yourself to follow his plan for Christian marriage? Explain.

Leader's Notes

Question 2. Song of Songs is love poetry. Another translation of verse 1 is "Song of All Songs," which is the Hebrew idiom meaning "the best of all songs." According to verse 1, Solomon was the author. He is named six other times in the book and is referred to as "the king" five times. Solomon probably wrote this book during his reign as king of Israel (971–931 B.C.).

Question 3. Apparently the setting is King Solomon's court from the viewpoint of the bride. She sounds more like a young lover than a bride, but the songs fit the character and customs of an ancient Middle Eastern wedding. Brides commonly were in their teens. In this song, the bride often takes the initiative. She calls her bridegroom "king" (Song of Songs 1:4,12). Later we find he is Solomon (3:11).

Question 6. The bride was dark because, as a country girl, she was more sunburned than city girls were. She is identified as a Shulammite (6:13), that is, from the village of Shulem on the Plain of Esdraelon. "Daughters of Jerusalem" (1:5) were female wedding guests, close friends of the bride. "A veiled woman" (1:7) was a roadside prostitute.

Question 8. This question helps us bridge the gap between ancient and modern times and customs. Although God is not mentioned in Song of Songs, we must think about his place in courtship and marriage according to New Testament standards and values.

Question 9. Women commonly wore small pouches of perfume around their necks (1:12-13). Henna blossoms were considered the loveliest of flowers, and En Gedi was a luxuriant oasis on the western edge of the Dead Sea (1:14).

Question 10. This marks the beginning of the first extended conversation between bride and bridegroom.

Reflections. Budget your time to allow at least five minutes for these questions. Encourage wide participation. There are no right and wrong answers to these questions.

STUDY 2: INTIMACY REFRESHED

Question 2. The bride sees herself as her bridegroom sees her. The rose was a member of the crocus family, perhaps a daffodil. Sharon was the coastal plain in north central Israel.

Question 3. This conversational interplay is suggested by the *New English Bible:* "No, a lily among thorns is my dearest among girls."

Question 4. The banner was a battle flag used to muster the troops and give directions. This imagery signifies a public declaration of the bridegroom's love.

Question 5. "Every girl who falls in love should find such rest in the one she loves. And she should find such rest in no one else" (S. Craig Glickman, *A Song for Lovers,* Downers Grove, Ill.: InterVarsity, 1976, p. 40). She loves him so much that she wants him to embrace her.

Question 6. The desire for physical love is normal in courtship. Restraint is healthy, beneficial, and follows biblical standards.

Question 8. The bridegroom not only uses words of endearment, but he also emphasizes their personal relationship: "Come with me."

Question 9. "One good indication of real love is the desire to communicate, a wish to discover all about this person whom you love so much" (Glickman, *A Song for Lovers,* p. 47).

Question 10. The command in 2:15 may be directed against something interfering with the lovers. Many things can ruin love and intimacy: mistrust, jealousy, pride, selfishness, an unforgiving spirit.

Question 11. "He browses" means "he pastures his flock," a picture of the bridegroom fulfilling his shepherd's role.

Question 13. Poets and lyricists have long used the love story of Song of Songs to refer to Jesus and his beloved. "Jesus, lover of my soul" is one example. He is called the lily of the valley and the rose of Sharon in various hymns. "His Banner Over Me Is Love" is another example. "I am his and he is mine" is the refrain of the hymn "Loved with Everlasting Love." The New Testament also calls the church the bride of Christ. See Ephesians 5:22-33 and Revelation 19:6-8.

Study 3: Intimacy Desired

Question 5. Allow time for people to recall similar plots. Come prepared with some you have read or seen. You may need to prime the group with your contributions.

Question 6. The bride's home represented security to her. It was a safe place. This would alleviate her fears. Also, this would symbolically bind her future lovemaking to that of her parents. (See 8:2,5.)

Question 7. We find similar warnings throughout Scripture: "You shall not commit adultery" (Exodus 20:14); "With persuasive words she led him astray...do not let your heart turn to her ways or stray into her paths" (Proverbs 7:21,25); "For from within, out of men's hearts, come evil thoughts, sexual immorality, adultery..." (Mark 7:21); "Flee from sexual immorality" (1 Corinthians 6:18); "Flee the evil desires of youth" (2 Timothy 2:22).

Question 9. The wedding procession focused on the bridegroom, not the bride. This full-dress military wedding showed the king's power and importance. Symbolically, it pointed to his protection and provision for his bride.

Question 11. The best wood for making furniture came from the hills of Lebanon. Gold and silver came from the king's treasury. Purple cloth (3:10) signified royalty. Perhaps the king's friends helped him, just as mothers help their daughters prepare for the wedding ceremony today.

STUDY 4: INTIMACY DESCRIBED

Question 2. The bridegroom's metaphors for his love's beauty express profound feelings. He searches for the right words, which fit within the context of his culture. To him, the picture of a flock of goats streaming down the mountain reminds him of his bride's hair. The fawns remind him of her breasts; the whiteness of the sheep, of her teeth. Her temples include her cheeks, tinged with the redness of the pomegranate. Her neck speaks to him of the strength and integrity of King David's fortress.

Question 4. By this time your group members will probably feel comfortable with one another. Allow time for reflection, and pray for and encourage honest responses.

Question 5. References to mountains (Lebanon, Amana, Senir, Hermon), lions, and leopards are a poetic way of drawing the bride from fear to security with the bridegroom.

Question 6. One glance at her eyes is enough to excite the bridegroom (4:9). He calls her "sister," a cultural term of affection for one's wife. "Milk and honey" (4:11) was the normal expression for the abundance and blessing of the land.

Question 8. The bridegroom uses the garden as an extended metaphor (4:12,15,16). He names several spring flowers and valuable spices. His garden first has a sealed fountain, which becomes a gushing fountain that enriches the whole land. The "garden locked up" (4:12) refers to the bride's virginity.

Question 9. The bride picks up the bridegroom's metaphor of her love as a garden, which she opened to him on their wedding night.

STUDY 5: INTIMACY ANTICIPATED

Question 2. See how the poet brings in the couple's friends to encourage their lovemaking. Some interpreters attribute these words to God, thus giving divine approval to sex in marriage.

Question 4. "My lover is knocking" indicates separate bedrooms in the royal palace. The bridegroom has used the endearing terms of "sister, darling, dove, and flawless one" before, but this is the first time he uses them all together. "My flawless one" may also be translated "my treasure." "Dew" and "dampness" may indicate that he had been out late on business, or else he just got caught in the rain.

Question 6. Aim for personal, not theoretical answers. Because some group members may be shy about talking openly about such matters, allow for quiet reflection. We don't want trite contributions. Laughter is also good medicine when discussing these things.

Question 7. Perhaps she rushed out improperly clothed and was mistaken for a thief. Imagine the watchmen's reactions when they discovered she was the queen.

Question 9. This is a sensitive issue, but the New Testament instructs us to encourage one another and to bear one another's burdens (Galatians 6:2; Ephesians 4:2; Hebrews 3:13; 10:25). It also enjoins us to speak the truth in love (Ephesians 4:15).

STUDY 6: INTIMACY RECOVERED

Question 2. The identification of speakers and the meaning of several Hebrew words in this section have troubled scholars, some of whom say this is the toughest chapter in Song of Songs. We follow the identification scheme of the *New International Version* throughout, but we also suggest some others.

Question 4. Because our lovers' songs in this chapter repeat earlier passionate songs, allow extended time for reading and discussion of these foundational texts for the Christian understanding of marriage.

Question 5. Tirzah (6:4) later became the place of the palace of Israel's kings, just as Jerusalem was for Judah's kings (1 Kings 15:33).

Question 7. Cultural norms permitted multiple wives and concubines, so this bride's uniqueness was special indeed. God warned the Israelites against marrying foreign women, knowing that pagan religions would infect his people. When Solomon broke this law, his faith and his devotion to the Lord suffered (1 Kings 11:1-13).

Question 8. Encourage frank answers. Give people time to think and respond. Avoid starting with your own ideas.

Question 9. Other Bible versions assign Song of Songs 6:11-12 to the bride. "Chariots of my people" may read "chariots of Amminadib," a kind of royal chariot, or palanquin, carried by willing men.

Question 10. Songs of Songs 6:13 has also been divided this way: *Friends:* "Come back, come back." *Bride:* "Why would you gaze on the Shulammite?" Apparently "to gaze on you" meant to see her dance. "Why do you want to look at me where there are so many others in this dance?" (C. Lloyd Carr, *The Song of Solomon,* InterVarsity, 1984, p. 155). *Mahanaim* is Hebrew for the "dance of two armies." In the Hebrew Bible, chapter 7 begins with 6:13.

Question 11. Our questions about "scenes" do not mean that Song of Songs was written as a drama. It is a collection of poetic love songs without a plot. But it helps us to visualize the emotional themes in these songs as an ongoing drama. Scholars have written copiously about who the singers are and where the breaks should come. Nevertheless, Song of Songs is impossible to outline as a linear story.

STUDY 7: INTIMACY FULFILLED

Question 3. Regarding this explicit description, Glickman observes, "It is all part of their lovemaking, and God does not stutter to describe it" (*A Song for Lovers,* p. 83). However, Bible translators stutter when trying to figure out what some of the Hebrew words mean. For example, "graceful legs" (Song of Songs 7:1) can also read "rounded thighs" or "curve of your thighs." And "waist" (7:2) means "her belly below her navel."

Bible commentators also suggest possible symbolism. For

example, "Your neck is like an ivory tower" may represent noble dignity or artistic smoothness. Her eyes are like "the pools of Heshbon by the gate of Bath Rabbim" (7:4). Bath Rabbim is an unknown city, but it may stand for a hurried, busy city life. If so, her eyes would speak of quiet refreshment. Some commentators see the strength of her character reflected in the metaphor of her nose: "like the tower of Lebanon" (7:4). Prominent noses were not considered beautiful. Beautiful noses were noted for their color, not their size or shape. "Damascus" (7:4) represents the Syrian enemy, so perhaps the tower was a metaphor of protection.

Question 4. "Your delights" (7:6) looks back to past lovemaking and thus inspires his anticipation of more in the future.

Question 5. Discuss the themes of the lyrics people hear on the radio and CDs as well as the sexual mores reflected on television today.

Question 6. The bridegroom's mention of wine inspires the bride to interrupt with her own interpretation of his metaphor. The term for "teeth" is a problematic translation of the Hebrew. One alternative reading is "lips of sleepers." If so, it may mean that their lovemaking is over, and they will go to sleep. In this case, her song then resumes the next morning.

Question 7. Read these verses several times to note the different ways the bride expresses her relationship to her bridegroom.

Question 8. Ephesians 5:21 is a basic Christian truth undergirding successful marriages. Perhaps this concept will be new to some people. Allow time for questions. Think through how you can summarize the discussion.

Question 10. Mandrakes (7:13), or love apples, were well known and widely used as an aphrodisiac. "Every delicacy," such as choice fruits, is her metaphor for her physical, erotic attractions.

Question 12. Think about general biblical principles related to living in marriage according to God's perfect will. We obey and glorify him as we demonstrate the oneness he intended and as we express this oneness in our emotional, spiritual, and physical love.

STUDY 8: INTIMACY MATURED

Question 2. She sees the bridegroom as her brother and lover. Public displays of affection were avoided except among family members. The bride wishes her bridegroom were like her brother so that it would be acceptable for her to display her affection for him at any time. She assumes the roles of his older sister and even his mother.

Spiced wine and nectar have erotic connotations (verse 2). Song of Songs 8:3 is a reprise of 2:6.

Question 4. A seal in ancient times was generally used to indicate ownership of a person's valued possessions. They were engraved on stone or metal. The bride wants to own her bridegroom's affections (heart) and his deeds (arm).

Question 5. The word *strong* refers to either an irresistible assailant or an immovable defense. *Jealousy* is not a pejorative term here; rather, it means the rightful claim of possession. The comparison "as strong as death…as the grave" refers to the fact that just as the grave does not give up the dead, so her bridegroom will not give up his bride.

Question 8. The phrase "she is spoken for" refers to future marriage. The wall and door symbolize strength and security.

Question 9. Peace and contentment (8:10) are mentioned nine times in this song, showing how much joy can be found in marital intimacy.

Apparently the vineyard (8:11-12) was where they had met (1:6). Her vineyard represents her own person; she gives the value of her person to her bridegroom. In ancient times, vinedressers were supposed to give the owner one thousand shekels and receive two hundred shekels in wages.

Question 10. The bridegroom wants to grow in his knowledge of the bride, showing this aspect of maturing intimacy. She longs to make love, showing continuing fulfillment of God's purposes in marriage. "Come away" means to make haste. The word is used in the Old Testament for flight from enemy armies. "Spice-laden mountain" speaks of their physical union.

Question 12. Allow ample time for thoughtful reflection.

Question 13. The purpose of this question is to discover that their intimacy was more than purely sexual. Wait for specific responses. Don't settle for vague generalities.

What Should We Study Next?

To help your group answer that question, we've listed the Fisherman studyguides by category so you can choose your next study.

TOPICAL STUDIES

Angels by Vinita Hampton Wright

Becoming Women of Purpose by Ruth Haley Barton

Building Your House on the Lord: Marriage and Parenthood by Steve and Dee Brestin

The Creative Heart of God: Living with Imagination by Ruth Goring

Discipleship: The Growing Christian's Lifestyle by James and Martha Reapsome

Doing Justice, Showing Mercy: Christian Actions in Today's World by Vinita Hampton Wright

Encouraging Others: Biblical Models for Caring by Lin Johnson

The End Times: Discovering What the Bible Says by E. Michael Rusten

Examining the Claims of Jesus by Dee Brestin

Friendship: Portraits in God's Family Album by Steve and Dee Brestin

The Fruit of the Spirit: Growing in Christian Character by Stuart Briscoe

Great Doctrines of the Bible by Stephen Board

Great Passages of the Bible by Carol Plueddemann

Great Prayers of the Bible by Carol Plueddemann

Growing Through Life's Challenges by James and Martha
Reapsome

Guidance & God's Will by Tom and Joan Stark

Heart Renewal: Finding Spiritual Refreshment by Ruth
Goring

Higher Ground: Steps Toward Christian Maturity by Steve
and Dee Brestin

*Images of Redemption: God's Unfolding Plan Through the
Bible* by Ruth Van Reken

Integrity: Character from the Inside Out by Ted Engstrom
and Robert Larson

Lifestyle Priorities by John White

Marriage: Learning from Couples in Scripture by R. Paul
and Gail Stevens

Miracles by Robbie Castleman

One Body, One Spirit: Building Relationships in the Church
by Dale and Sandy Larsen

The Parables of Jesus by Gladys Hunt

Parenting with Purpose and Grace by Alice Fryling

Prayer: Discovering What the Bible Says by Timothy Jones
and Jill Zook-Jones

The Prophets: God's Truth Tellers by Vinita Hampton
Wright

Proverbs and Parables: God's Wisdom for Living by Dee
Brestin

Satisfying Work: Christian Living from Nine to Five
by R. Paul Stevens and Gerry Schoberg

Senior Saints: Growing Older in God's Family by James and
Martha Reapsome

The Sermon on the Mount: The God Who Understands Me by Gladys Hunt

Spiritual Gifts by Karen Dockrey

Spiritual Hunger: Filling Your Deepest Longings by Jim and Carol Plueddemann

A Spiritual Legacy: Faith for the Next Generation by Chuck and Winnie Christensen

Spiritual Warfare by A. Scott Moreau

The Ten Commandments: God's Rules for Living by Stuart Briscoe

Ultimate Hope for Changing Times by Dale and Sandy Larsen

Who Is God? by David P. Seemuth

Who Is Jesus? In His Own Words by Ruth Van Reken

Who Is the Holy Spirit? by Barbara Knuckles and Ruth Van Reken

Wisdom for Today's Woman: Insights from Esther by Poppy Smith

Witnesses to All the World: God's Heart for the Nations by Jim and Carol Plueddemann

Women at Midlife: Embracing the Challenges by Jeanie Miley

Worship: Discovering What Scripture Says by Larry Sibley

BIBLE BOOK STUDIES

Genesis: Walking with God by Margaret Fromer and Sharrel Keyes

Exodus: God Our Deliverer by Dale and Sandy Larsen

Ruth: Relationships That Bring Life by Ruth Haley Barton

Ezra and Nehemiah: A Time to Rebuild by James Reapsome
(For Esther, see Topical Studies, *Wisdom for Today's Woman*)
Job: Trusting Through Trials by Ron Klug
Psalms: A Guide to Prayer and Praise by Ron Klug
Proverbs: Wisdom That Works by Vinita Hampton Wright
Ecclesiastes: A Time for Everything by Stephen Board
Jeremiah: The Man and His Message by James Reapsome
Jonah, Habakkuk, and Malachi: Living Responsibly
     by Margaret Fromer and Sharrel Keyes
Matthew: People of the Kingdom by Larry Sibley
Mark: God in Action by Chuck and Winnie Christensen
Luke: Following Jesus by Sharrel Keyes
John: The Living Word by Whitney Kuniholm
Acts 1–12: God Moves in the Early Church by Chuck and
     Winnie Christensen
Acts 13–28, see *Paul* under Character Studies
Romans: The Christian Story by James Reapsome
1 Corinthians: Problems and Solutions in a Growing Church
     by Charles and Ann Hummel
Strengthened to Serve: 2 Corinthians by Jim and Carol
     Plueddemann
Galatians, Titus, and Philemon: Freedom in Christ
     by Whitney Kuniholm
Ephesians: Living in God's Household by Robert Baylis
Philippians: God's Guide to Joy by Ron Klug
Colossians: Focus on Christ by Luci Shaw
Letters to the Thessalonians by Margaret Fromer and
     Sharrel Keyes
Letters to Timothy: Discipleship in Action by Margaret
     Fromer and Sharrel Keyes
Hebrews: Foundations for Faith by Gladys Hunt

James: Faith in Action by Chuck and Winnie Christensen

1 and 2 Peter, Jude: Called for a Purpose by Steve and Dee Brestin

How Should a Christian Live? 1, 2, and 3 John by Dee Brestin

Revelation: The Lamb Who Is a Lion by Gladys Hunt

BIBLE CHARACTER STUDIES

Abraham: Model of Faith by James Reapsome

David: Man After God's Own Heart by Robbie Castleman

Elijah: Obedience in a Threatening World by Robbie Castleman

Great People of the Bible by Carol Plueddemann

King David: Trusting God for a Lifetime by Robbie Castleman

Men Like Us: Ordinary Men, Extraordinary God by Paul Heidebrecht and Ted Scheuermann

Moses: Encountering God by Greg Asimakoupoulos

Paul: Thirteenth Apostle (Acts 13–28) by Chuck and Winnie Christensen

Women Like Us: Wisdom for Today's Issues by Ruth Haley Barton

Women Who Achieved for God by Winnie Christensen

Women Who Believed God by Winnie Christensen